Sensible Shoes

JOURNAL

Sharon Garlough Brown

An imprint of InterVarsity Press
Downers Grove, Illinois

InterVarsity Press
P.O. Box 1400, Downers Grove, IL 60515-1426
ivpress.com
email@ivpress.com

InterVarsity Press® is the book-publishing division of InterVarsity Christian Fellowship/USA®, a movement of students and faculty active on campus at hundreds of universities, colleges, and schools of nursing in the United States of America, and a member movement of the International Fellowship of Evangelical Students. For information about local and regional activities, visit intervarsity.org.

Cover design and image composite: Beth McGill
Interior design: Daniel van Loon
Images: wheat field © Yufan Sun / EyeEm / Getty Images
      green field © Xuanyu Han / Moment Collection / Getty Images

ISBN 978-0-8308-4690-0 (print)

Printed in the United States of America ♾

InterVarsity Press is committed to ecological stewardship and to the conservation of natural resources in all our operations. This book was printed using sustainably sourced paper.

Library of Congress Cataloging-in-Publication Data
A catalog record for this book is available from the Library of Congress.

P	21	20	19	18	17	16	15	14	13	12	11	10	9	8	7	6	5	4	3	2	1
Y	37	36	35	34	33	32	31	30	29	28	27	26	25	24	23	22	21	20			

Welcome

$\mathcal{I}$'m always delighted when a reader wants to show me a marked-up copy of *Sensible Shoes*, with underlined passages, dog-eared pages, or index tabs marking memorable lines. For this journal I've selected fifty quotes that invite reflection, provide encouragement, or serve as prompts for prayer. Rather than present the quotes chronologically from the book, I've curated them according to themes that emerge from the characters' journeys.

Katherine gives this advice as they begin their retreat: "Keep a travelogue of your pilgrimage. I'm confident the Holy Spirit will be revealing many things as you take the time to slow down, be still, and listen." I hope these pages will provide space for you to "stay with what stirs you" and be drawn ever deeper into the heart of God.

Grace and joy to you in the journey!

> *Walking the path toward freedom and deep transformation takes courage. It's not easy. It's not linear. It can seem messy and chaotic at times, and you're likely to lose your sense of equilibrium as old things die and new things are born. But don't be afraid of the mess.*
>
> KATHERINE

> The Lord shepherds
> gently, always with
> a loving and steady
> hand. So just take the
> journey one step at
> a time, inviting and
> trusting God to bring
> to the surface what is
> ready to be healed.
>
> KATHERINE

Much as we might wish to direct our own spiritual journeys, growing in love for God and others is a lifelong process that can't be achieved by self-effort. We've got to learn how to cooperate with the Holy Spirit.

NATHAN

> *You begin the journey
> with a wonderful gift if
> you already know you
> are poor in spirit—if
> you already see how
> desperately you need
> God. Humility is always
> the starting place for
> those who want to
> draw near to God.*
>
> KATHERINE

> We don't need to retreat to a far-off place or abandon our daily lives to encounter God. But we do need training in how to discern the movement of God's Spirit in ordinary and everyday circumstances.
>
> KATHERINE

The spiritual life is all
about paying attention.
The Spirit of God is
always speaking to
us, but we need to
get off autopilot and
take time to look and
listen with the eyes
and ears of the heart.

KATHERINE

> The intent of spiritual disciplines is to create space where we can encounter God—space where we can be deeply touched and changed by God's extravagant love for us.
>
> KATHERINE

> *We don't have the power to make the sun rise, but we can choose to be awake when it happens. Spiritual disciplines help us stay awake.*
>
> DAWN

We need designated time for stillness and listening. It takes time to identify the baggage we've been carrying that weighs us down.

KATHERINE

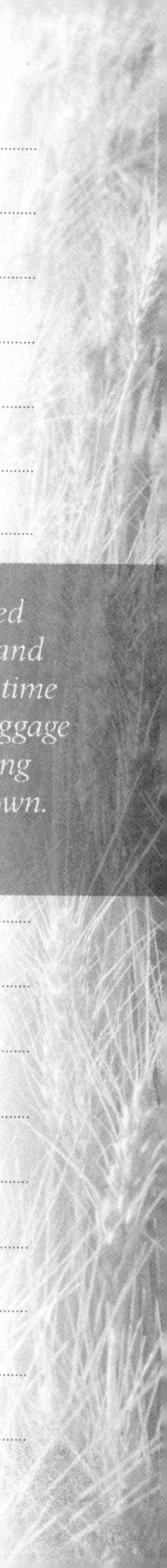

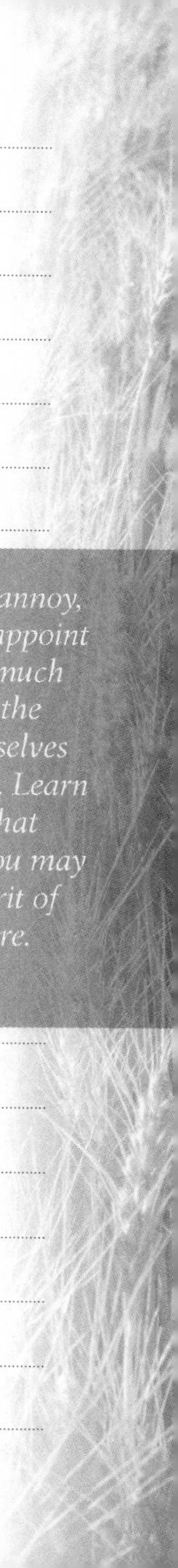

The things that annoy, irritate, and disappoint us have just as much power to reveal the truth about ourselves as anything else. Learn to linger with what provokes you. You may just find the Spirit of God moving there.

NATHAN

God's grace is so big that even our weaknesses become wonderful opportunities for the Spirit to work in us. Our fears, our temptations— even our sins—can draw us closer to God.

KATHERINE

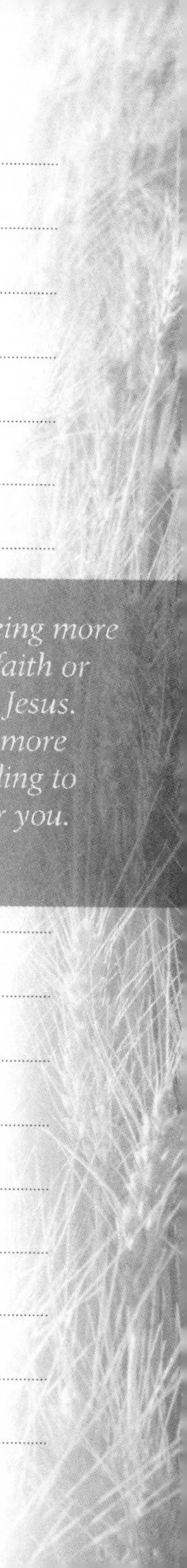

It's not about being more perfect in your faith or in your love for Jesus. It's about being more open to responding to his deep love for you.

NATHAN

> *The spiritual life is a journey, not an exam.*
>
> NATHAN

> *Jesus loves you too much to let you root your identity in what you do for him, rather than who you are to him. He loves you too much to let you wrap yourself in anything other than his love for you—his deep, uncontainable, extravagant love for you.*
>
> KATHERINE

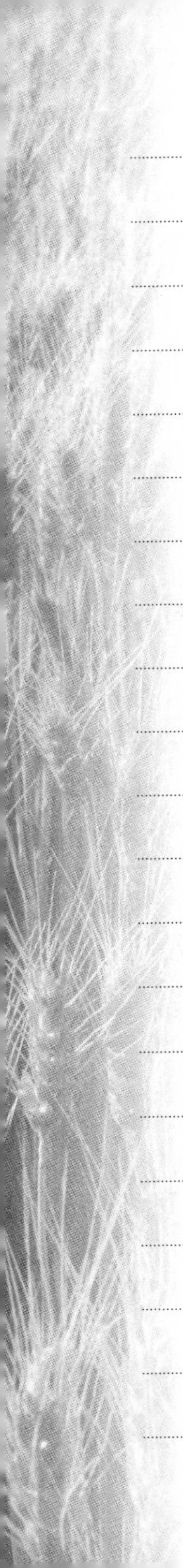

Let go of trying to purify your own love for God and just let this be a season of exploring how deeply God treasures you. Let this be a time of being open and receptive to Jesus pouring his love into you, apart from anything you do for him.

KATHERINE

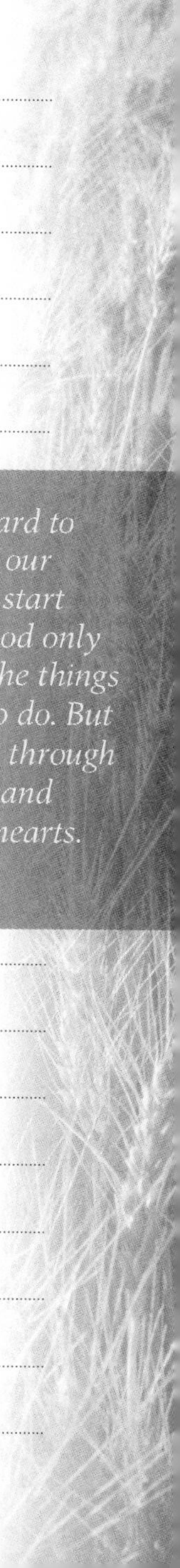

Sometimes it's hard to pay attention to our own desires. We start believing that God only wants us to do the things we don't want to do. But God also speaks through the deep desires and longings of our hearts.

KATHERINE

God is always the first one to move in his relationship with us. Our movement is always a response to the Love which loved us first.

NATHAN

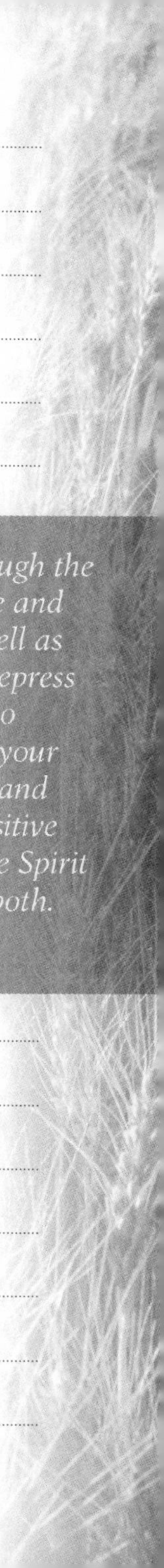

God speaks through the things that excite and energize us as well as the things that depress and deplete us. So pay attention to your strong reactions and feelings, both positive and negative. The Spirit speaks through both.

KATHERINE

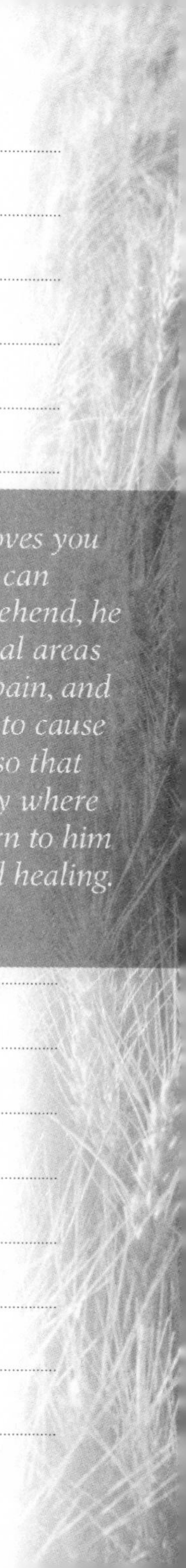

Because God loves you more than you can possibly comprehend, he will gently reveal areas of discomfort, pain, and agitation—not to cause you harm, but so that you can identify where it hurts and turn to him for comfort and healing.

KATHERINE

God never says, "Just get over it." God says, "Give it to me."

KATHERINE

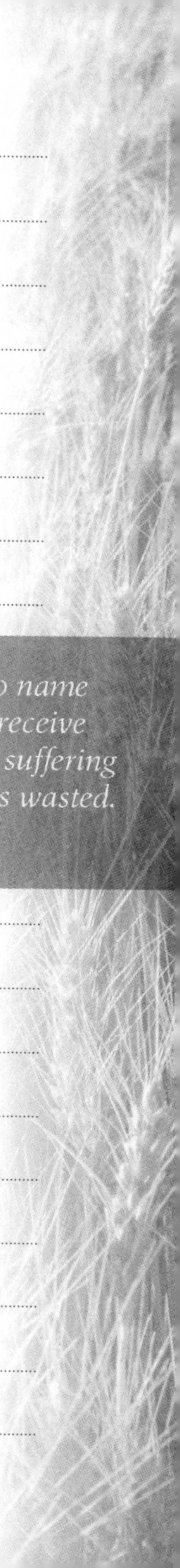

Jesus invites us to name our pain and to receive his grace for our suffering so that nothing is wasted.

KATHERINE

> *It takes courage to grieve well, and God is able to give you the courage.*
>
> KATHERINE

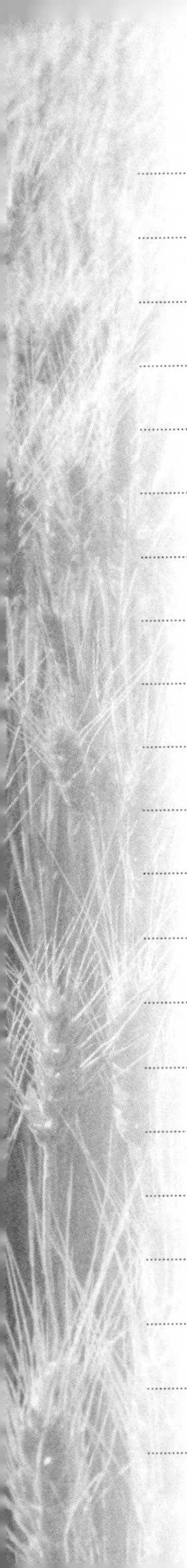

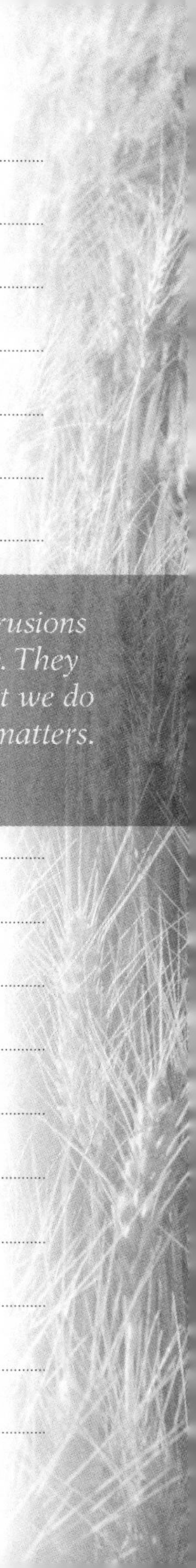

Life's painful intrusions aren't negotiable. They happen. It's what we do with them that matters.

KATHERINE

Let your fears do the hard work of revealing deep truths about yourself. Our fears can be windows into the raw and unvarnished truth of our lives. We don't cling to them or feed them, but we do listen prayerfully to what they teach us.

KATHERINE

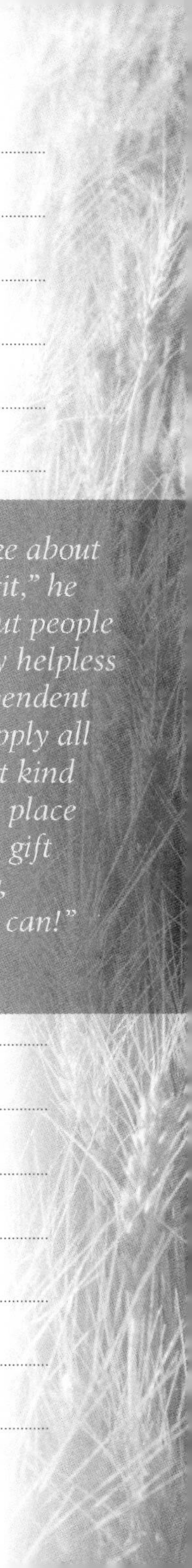

When Jesus spoke about the "poor in spirit," he was talking about people who were totally helpless and entirely dependent upon God to supply all their needs. That kind of weakness is a place of blessing. It's a gift to be able to say, "I can't, but God can!"

KATHERINE

> *Faith isn't about not being afraid. Faith means we trust God, even when we're afraid.*
>
> KATHERINE

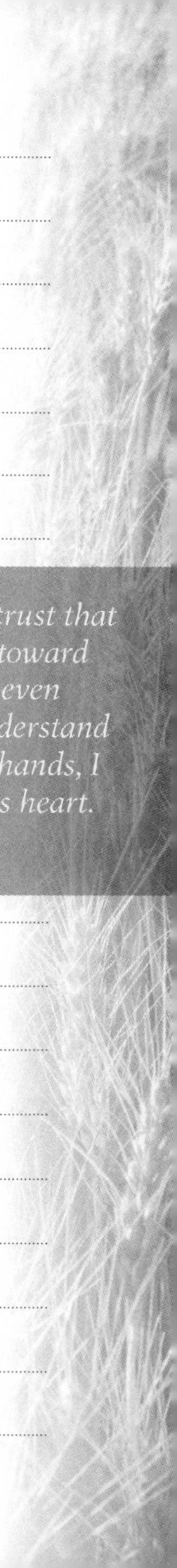

If I can always trust that God's intention toward me is love, then even when I don't understand the work of his hands, I can still trust his heart.

NATHAN

> Where have you come from? Where are you going? As we pursue deep transformation in Christ, we need to name and contemplate what has shaped us in the past. We also need to consider how we are moving forward in our life with God.
>
> KATHERINE

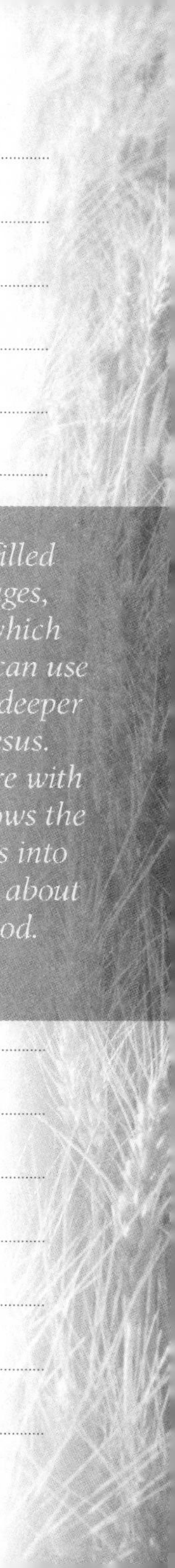

Our minds are filled with stories, images, and memories which the Holy Spirit can use to bring us into deeper intimacy with Jesus. Praying Scripture with imagination allows the Spirit to guide us into places of insight about ourselves and God.

KATHERINE

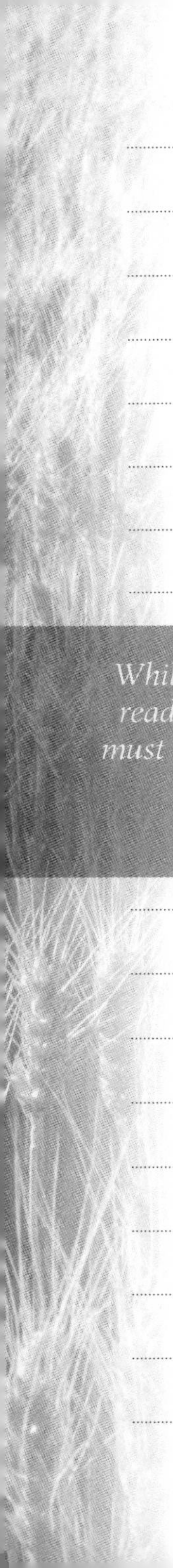

While it's essential to read God's Word, we must also allow God's Word to read us.

KATHERINE

It's a gift when the Holy Spirit exposes areas of darkness, captivity, and sin. When you can actually see the ugliness, it's because the light has come, revealing what was already there.

KATHERINE

> *The exposure of sin is the beginning of its destruction.*
>
> KATHERINE

Ask for the courage to be uncomfortable, uneasy, and provoked so you can confess and release these things. The Lord is full of compassion and love for you. God wants to reveal truth so that the truth sets you free.

KATHERINE

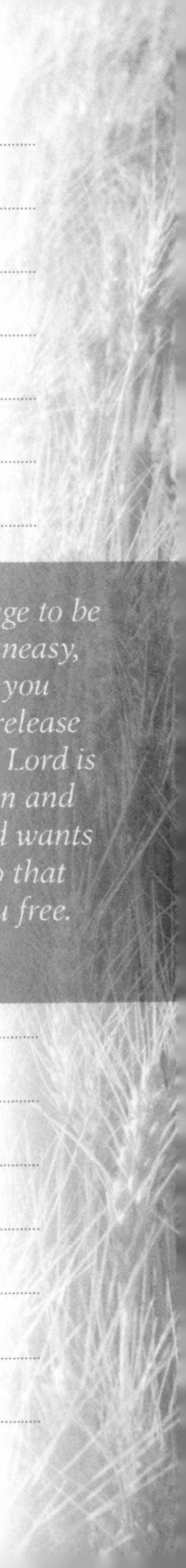

Self-examination isn't about being perfect. It's about listening and responding to the Spirit. It's about allowing God to reveal where we are hiding and resisting his love so that we can come out from hiding to receive grace and mercy and wholeness.

KATHERINE

> There's such freedom in being able to say, "Yes, that's my sin. And yes, I have a Savior." No need to hide. No need to be defensive. No need to be ashamed. No need to carry the burden of trying to be perfect.
>
> KATHERINE

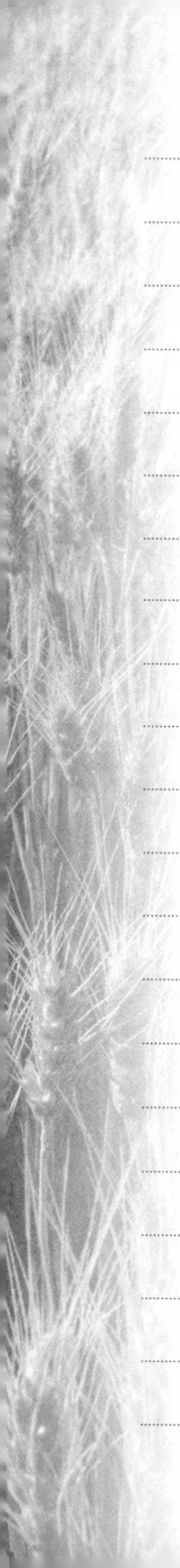

It's hard for a good
rule follower to be
converted to grace. There
are so many defenses
we perfectionists hide
behind, especially the
impulse to trust our own
efforts to live rightly and
faithfully. It's not your
goodness that saves you.
Or your performance.
It's grace. All grace.

NATHAN

> *The only way you could disappoint God would be if God had an unrealistic, idealized view of you. And God does not. There are many things the Lord desires for us. But his desires for us are rooted in his love and longing for us. Not in disappointment and condemnation.*
>
> KATHERINE

> *God didn't choose you out of pity. Jesus really has chosen you to be with him because he loves you and wants to be with you.*
>
> DAWN

> Let everything you see
> about Jesus begin to
> reshape your image of
> God and your image
> of yourself. God is love.
> And you are chosen,
> accepted, loved, forgiven,
> and treasured. That's
> how El Roi sees you.
> You are God's beloved.
>
> KATHERINE

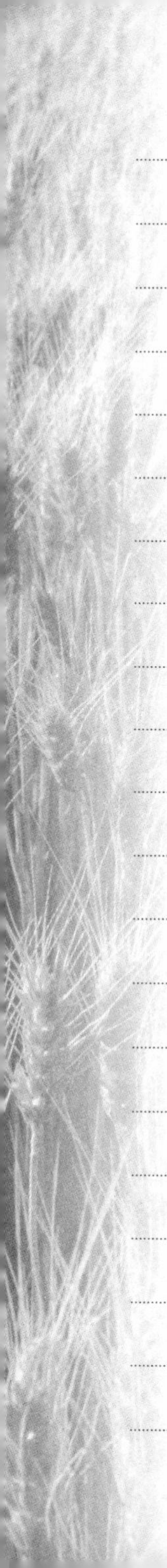

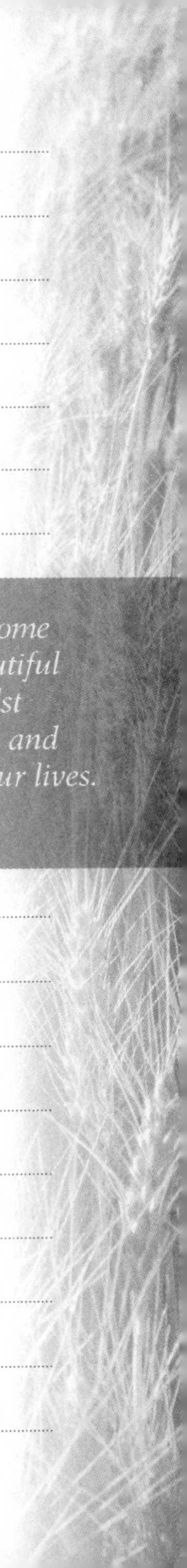

The Lord does some of his most beautiful work in the midst of the messiness and brokenness of our lives.

KATHERINE

We can't make ourselves whole or holy. That's the Spirit's work. Our work is simply to cooperate with the Spirit by saying yes to God's movement in our lives.

KATHERINE

> *Spiritual disciplines are all about forming new habits and new rhythms. If you've mastered the "I can't" part, then you can start practicing the second part along with it: "The Lord can."*
>
> KATHERINE

> *It's easy to lose sight of how far I've come if I'm only looking at how far I have to go.*
>
> MEG

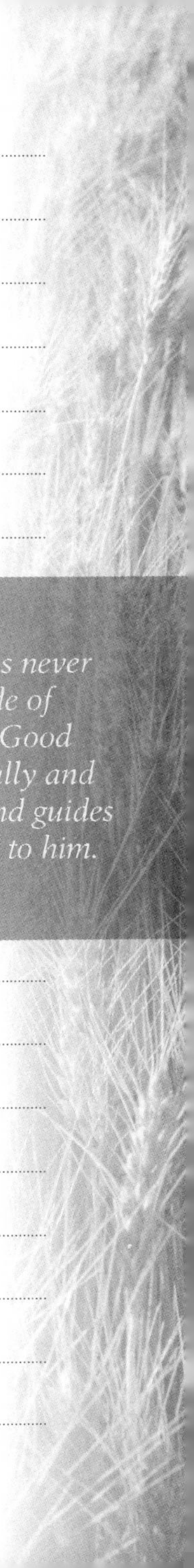

The process of transformation is never complete this side of heaven. But the Good Shepherd faithfully and lovingly leads and guides us as we say yes to him.

KATHERINE

My way forward is
always about going
deeper into God's love
for me, deeper into union
and communion with
him. I'm walking the
road to claiming my
identity as the beloved
of God. Nothing more,
nothing less. And that
hasn't been an easy or
straightforward journey.
But I'm getting there.

NATHAN

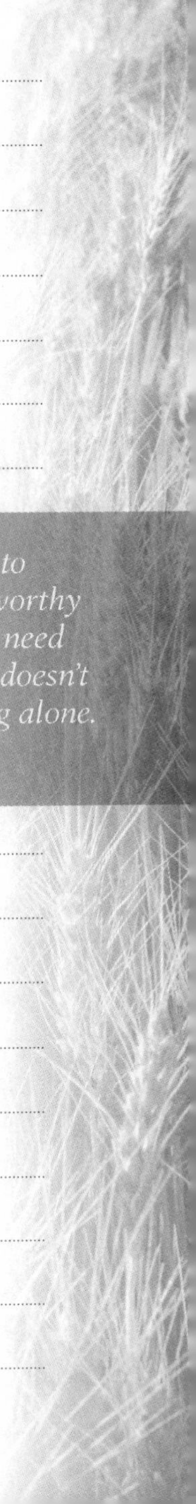

It's a special gift to walk with trustworthy companions. We need each other. God doesn't want us traveling alone.

KATHERINE

> *Even though we sometimes experience significant breakthroughs and tangible evidence of the Spirit's work in our lives, spiritual growth is often imperceptible. I encourage you to be patient.*
>
> KATHERINE

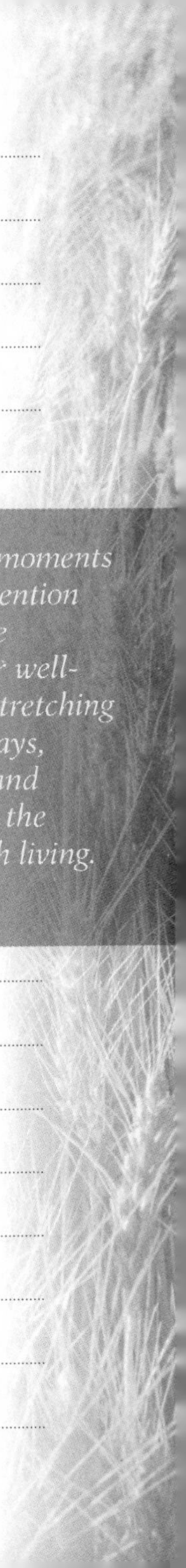

When we string moments of God-ward attention together, soon we discover that our well-lived hours are stretching into well-lived days, weeks, months, and years. And that's the kind of life worth living.

KATHERINE

Always remember. The flowers are for you.

HANNAH

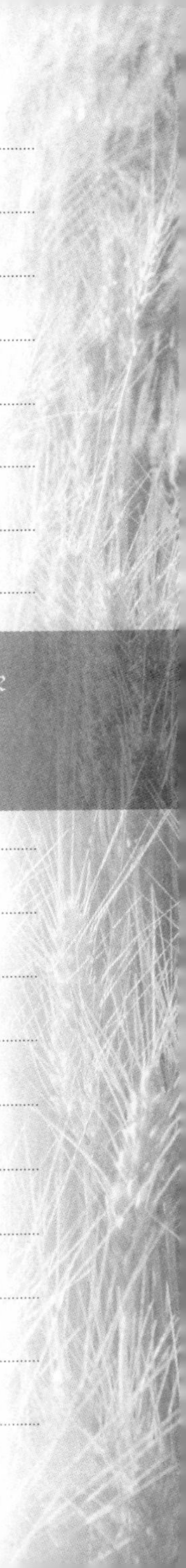

My beloved, walk with me.

HANNAH

The Sensible Shoes Series

Sensible Shoes
SERIES
Sharon Garlough Brown
Sensible Shoes
Two Steps Forward
Barefoot
An Extra Mile
Brown

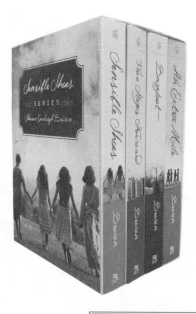

Sensible Shoes
Two Steps Forward
Barefoot
An Extra Mile

STUDY GUIDES

Sensible Shoes
STUDY GUIDE
Sharon Garlough Brown
Two Steps Forward
STUDY GUIDE
Sharon Garlough Brown
Barefoot
STUDY GUIDE
Sharon Garlough Brown
An Extra Mile
STUDY GUIDE
Sharon Garlough Brown

For more information about the Sensible Shoes series,
visit ivpress.com/sensibleshoesseries.
To learn more from Sharon Garlough Brown or to sign up for her newsletter,
visit sharongarloughbrown.com